David

AND HIS GOD

A Study through David's life and the Psalms.

GLENNA DERBYSHIRE

To request permissions, contact the publisher at admin@TellTheKids.com

Paperback ISBN: 978-1-953935-07-6
Electronic Book-ISBN: 978-1-953935-08-3
Library of Congress Control Number: 2020924142

Edited by Diane Hamilton
Cover and Interior Design by Nick Zink
Interior Layout by Anna Derbyshire

Scripture quotations marked (NLT) are taken from the Holy Bible, New Living Translation, copyright ©1996, 2004, 2015 by Tyndale House Foundation. Used by permission of Tyndale House Publishers, a Division of Tyndale House Ministries, Carol Stream, Illinois 60188. All rights reserved.

Scripture quotations marked (TPT) are from The Passion Translation® Copyright © 2017, 2018 by Passion & Fire Ministries, Inc. Used by permission. All rights reserved. ThePassionTranslation.com

Scripture quotations marked (YBB) are from the Young Believer Bible Copyright © 2003 by Tyndale House Publishers, Inc., Wheaton Illinois 60189. Used by permission. All rights reserved.

Scriptures marked NIV are taken from the NEW INTERNATIONAL VERSION (NIV): Scripture taken from THE HOLY BIBLE, NEW INTERNATIONAL VERSION ® Copyright© 1973, 1978, 1984, 2011 by Biblica, Inc.™ Used by permission of Zondervan

Printed by Ingram Spark in the USA

Tell The KIDS LLC
7700 Skylake Drive
Fort Worth TX 76179

TellTheKids.com

FORWARD

Since I was a little girl I admired David. His stories continually thrill and encourage me to get to know the God he loved, praised and served his entire life. The Psalms of David are part of my worship experience and a source of encouragement, direction and inspiration in my life. David and His God is a byproduct of those two realities. My prayer is as you study David, and the Psalms which he wrote through his life experiences, that you will be encouraged to follow God with all your heart.

-Glenna Derbyshire

Each Week's Study Will Have The Following Components:

- [ ] Scriptural Mini-Biography Of David
- [ ] The Psalm Or Psalms Applicable For That Period Of Time
- [ ] Daily Questions To Answer

These Will Challenge The Student To:

- [ ] Learn Who God Is
- [ ] List Attributes Of God
- [ ] Listen To The Voice Of God
- [ ] Lean On God
- [ ] Laugh With The Joy God Brings
- [ ] Leap Out In Faith
- [ ] Follow God's Direction

TABLE OF CONTENTS

CHAPTER 1

God Chooses

I Samuel 15, 16 and Psalm 78

God sometimes asks his followers to do difficult things; things that they would prefer not to do. Samuel, God's prophet, is an example of a man who obeyed God through an extremely difficult situation. He anointed Saul the first king of Israel and continued as his spiritual advisor. After Saul failed to follow God's directions, God instructed Samuel to tell Saul the kingdom would be taken away because God had rejected him as king.

As Samuel mourned Saul's loss, God told him to stop mourning; it was time for action. God told Samuel to go to the household of Jesse and anoint the next king. Samuel protested, telling God that Saul would kill him if he found out. After further discussion, Samuel obeyed God and went to Bethlehem and the house of Jesse, who was from the tribe of Judah.

The people of Bethlehem were afraid when they saw Samuel and asked him what was wrong. He assured them that everything was all right and invited them to purify themselves and come to the sacrifice.

Jesse and his sons arrived. When Samuel saw Eliab, he was sure that he was the next king. But God said, "No." God pointed out that he doesn't make decisions the way men do. Man looks at the outward appearance, God looks at the man's heart and thoughts. God's prophet

1

then summoned six more sons of Jesse with no success; God didn't want any of them.

Finally, he asked if Jesse had any other sons. Jesse replied, his youngest son, David, was in the fields watching the family's sheep. David was summoned from the fields and the Lord told Samuel he was the one. In the company of his family, David, a ruddy-faced handsome boy, was anointed King. From that day forward the Spirit of the Lord empowered him.

Day 1

Read Psalm 78:70-72

What does this story tell us about God?

Why didn't Samuel instantly obey God?

Are you sometimes reluctant to instantly obey God? Why?

Day 2

Read Psalm 78:1-8

It is important to not follow the example of the children of Israel found in Psalm 78:36-37, "but they followed him only with their words; they lied with their tongues. Their hearts were not loyal to him. They did not keep their covenant." (YBB) Instead we must hide God's words in our hearts following him with our minds and intellect: the place where our will and character originate.

What instructions does God give his people?

Why is it important for parents to follow this command?

Are there consequences for disobedience and if so, what are they?

What ways can you teach children in your life about God?

Day 3

Read Psalm 78

It is very important to teach our children and their children about God. Not just about David's God, but that his God loves them and that they can enjoy their own history with him.

As a child I often spent the night with my grandparents. Every morning we would kneel and pray and my grandfather would read from the Bible. I loved these special times with my grandparents.

My desire for my children and grand children is that they would listen and I will tell them about my walk with the Lord. I will share with them how God used his Word to encourage me, to correct me, to give me life.

List the names for God that you found

What do these names mean to you?

Look them up in a dictionary and record their meanings.

Day 4

Read Psalm 78

List the characteristics of God that you found.

According to this chapter God has emotions. List them.

Do these emotions change your view of God? How?

Day 5

Read Psalm 78

David expresses God as the God of miracles. Define a miracle.

List the miracles that you found in this passage.

Does one impress you more than another? If so, explain.

List the things about God in this chapter that make you want to praise and worship the Most High God.

Day 6

Write a prayer of thanksgiving and praise as you think about who God is.

Continue by asking for God's help and strength to help you obey the instructions you received from Psalm 78.

Day 7

You may be asking the questions I asked myself several times. "Why should Psalm 78 begin the study of David and His God?"

First, I selected it because the last three verses tell us God anointed David to be his King. Second, as I meditated on God's actions, I realized the revelation of God's power. And finally, I was amazed at the incredible lengths God took to show himself to his chosen people.

As I thought about what I wanted to accomplish through this study, I decided my main goal is for us to get to know God and how to follow his leadership in our lives. Solomon tells us in Proverbs, that the first step to becoming wise is to fear the Lord.

Therefore, our purpose is to get to know God, his attributes, his character and his desire for us to experience personally the great love he has for each one of us.

How can you apply this chapter to your life?

How has this chapter enlarged, enhanced or changed your view of God?

CHAPTER 2

God Prepares

I Samuel 17 and Psalm 139 and 144

God does wonderful things for us by creating us with talents and character traits that prepare us for his service. He did this for David in dramatic and exciting ways. In Chapter 1 of this study we learned David was taken from watching his father's sheep and anointed by Samuel, the Prophet of God to become the King of Israel. After his anointing, David continued shepherding the family's sheep.

King Saul searched for a skillful harpist to soothe him when overwhelmed by a tormenting spirit sent by God. A servant suggested David, who was able to soothe the king with his musical abilities. Saul promoted David, also known for bravery and strength, to a position as armor bearer.

Through this, David continued dividing his time between the sheep and the palace. One day David took food to his three older brothers who were fighting in Saul's army and a taunting giant piqued his curiosity. The Philistine was over nine feet tall and carried an enormous spear and a man went before him carrying a huge shield. David made inquiries and found that every day for a month Goliath had challenged the fighting men of Israel with these words, "Are you in need of a whole army to settle this? Choose someone to fight for you, and I will represent the Philistines. We will settle this dispute in single combat! If your man is able to kill me,

11

then we will be your slaves. But if I kill him, you will be our slaves! I defy the armies of Israel! Send me a man who will fight with me!" Saul's entire army of Israel was terrified.

David was not. He went to King Saul and told him he was Saul's man, and would kill the mighty nemesis. Saul told David he was a ridiculous boy and Goliath had trained since his youth. David persisted with a persuasive argument of how he killed bear and lion to protect sheep.

Saul wanted the Lord to be with David, and convinced David to wear his armor. When David tried to walk with Saul's armor it was evident the armor wouldn't work. He wasn't even able to walk! He removed Saul's armor and armed himself with a shepherd's bag in which he placed five smooth stones. He wielded his sling and went confidently to battle against the giant.

Goliath merely laughed when he saw the ruddy-faced boy coming to fight him. He cursed David in the name of his gods and promised birds and animals would eat his body.

David shouted his reply. "You come to me with sword, spear, and javelin, but I come in the name of the Lord Almighty—the God of the armies of Israel, whom you have defied. Today the Lord will conquer you, and I will sever your head. Then, I will give the dead bodies of your men to the birds and wild animals, and the entire world will know that there is a God in Israel. Everyone will know that the Lord does not need weapons to rescue his people. It is his battle, not ours. The Lord will give you to us."

After the war of words, they swiftly approached one another, ready for the battle to the death. David took a stone, put it in his sling, and let it fly. It hit Goliath directly in the forehead! Goliath fell face first to the ground, with a massive thud that shook the earth. David ran to Goliath's sword, pulled it from the sheath, and beheaded him. David's words proved true.

Day 1

A few years ago my husband was "between opportunities" and I was thinking about getting a job at a retail store. A friend of ours asked me to come to work for his insurance agency instead. He assured me he would teach me how to do everything I needed to do.

With fear and excitement I started my first job in over 20 years. It was quickly evident that God prepared me to handle this job. My math skills were honed by keeping score when I played games. Many years teaching women enriched my people skills. However, when it came time to make my first call to a government agency, I was terrified! I had no idea what to say. I prayed and then talked to myself and decided that the person at the other end of the phone would know what to do. So I made the call, and they did!

That wonderful job prepared me with confidence to try my current career of selling a technical product to government agencies at the highest level!

How did God prepare David his experience of killing a giant?

What was David's responsibility in this story?

What acts of service has God been preparing you to do?

Day 2

Read Psalms 139

List the names for God that you encountered in this chapter. Record the meaning of each name.   Look in a dictionary to find meanings of which you are unsure.

Record the verbs that describe God's ongoing relationship with David.

What uniquely human attributes does David tell his readers that God also possesses?

Day 3

Read Psalm 139

Psalm chapter 139 is filled with powerful and wonderful words! They have the power to transform lives when one understands and believes them. I am consistently overwhelmed and want to jump for joy when I read or think about how they tell me God is responsible for making me, me!

A group of new friends and I attended a retreat at a beautiful mountain camp. We decided to go for a walk at night to experience the "night shine" and witness the glories of a starlit night, without the interference of city lights. As we walked along, some began discussing what they didn't like about themselves. Finally I said, "I am fearfully and wonderfully made!" Soon they were all saying the words together. As truth penetrated hearts and minds, the tenor of the conversation changed from self-deprecation to gratitude. We thanked God for fearfully and wonderfully making each one uniquely special.

From Psalms 139: 1-6, describe ways God knows you.

Does this make you want to know him on a more intimate level?

What will you do to know him better?

Day 4

Read Psalms 139:7-12

Find the promises that these verses contain.

Have you ever tried to hide from God?

Compare and list parallels between Psalms 139:12 with I John 1:5.

Day 5

Before you read Psalms 139:13-18, ask God to open your eyes to see the words, open your ears to hear the words and open your heart to receive the truth of these words into your life.

Where was David's God while he was being formed and to what extent did God think about David?

How is God's personal interest in you expressed in this passage?

In what ways does the truth of God's incredible love for each of us impact you?

Psalm 139:17-18 profoundly impacts my life. I was thinking about them while I was on a business trip to California. I decided to get a pail and shovel and go to the beach. As I sat on the sand I thought about all the beaches I had visited. They were many: All of the U.S. coasts, shores in Hawaii, Thailand and Europe as well as Lake Michigan and many other lakes. I dipped my shovel in the sand and watched it slowly fall back to join the others, so many grains. It was overwhelming. I took a bucketful of sand home, filled a jar and affixed Psalm 139:17 and 18 to the front. It sits proudly on a shelf in my quiet room and continually reminds of God.

Day 6

Read Psalm 139:19-22

I have always hated the question, what was the author thinking when he included these thoughts? But I will ask this question, why do you think David included these verses in this wonderful chapter?

What grieved David and what do you think should grieve you?

According to Psalm 139:23-24, what did David invite God to do?

Is there anything in these verses you are prompted to invite God to do in your life?

Day 7

Read Psalm 144

David voiced these thoughts as he was facing Goliath the giant. Why did David say he loved God in verse one?

In Psalm 144:1 The Passion Translation contains five words that all start with the letter "S." Strong, safe, secure, describe the place God provides and the words strength and skill tell what God gives him to win the battle. How could this help you in your "Goliath" battles?

What questions does David ask God and what does he want God to do?

What did David promise to do in Psalm 144:9?

What blessings would happen as a result of David's deliverance and rescue by God?

Reread this chapter and record who David's God is.

How have these chapters enhanced, enlarged, or changed your view of God?

What things in these chapters made you want to jump for joy?

What steps of action did you take, or will you begin to take, as a result of studying God Prepares?

CHAPTER 3

God Protects

I Samuel 18, 19 and Psalm 31 and 59

Saul appointed David as a high-ranking army officer and he soon proved he was capable of the challenge. God was with David. He and his troops defeated all of their enemies.

Imagine being a king returning from a great victory greeted by throngs of women singing your praises. It would be wonderful! Now imagine the women are singing your praises but giving greater glory and honor to a young warrior. This happened to Saul. Each time the army of Israel returned from battle, the women danced and sang, "Saul slew thousands and David tens of thousands!" Saul did what most men would do. He grew angry, suspicious and jealous. He began watching David with a jaundiced eye.

David once again played the harp to soothe Saul with his music. Saul was toying with a spear and the evil spirit sent by God overwhelmed him. He hurled the spear at David trying to pin him to the wall. Not once, but two times! Both occasions God protected David and he was able to flee from Saul.

When Saul realized God left him and was now with David, he not only despised David's popularity but feared him as well. In an attempt to eliminate David the king made him commander of over a thousand men and sent David and his men into battle. However, the plan backfired. Once again David and his army defeated the enemy. David's popularity grew with each success as a warrior.

Michal, Saul's daughter, fell in love with the handsome nemesis of her father. When Saul found out, he was elated. Thinking that David could or would be killed in the process, Saul directed his attendants to inform David that he could be his son-in-law for the low price of 100 Philistine's foreskins. Once again the Lord was with David. He and his troops not only killed 100 of the enemy's men, they killed 200, and Michal became David's wife. However, the price was steep. Saul's anger, resentment and jealousy escalated until David was number one on his hit list.

Even so, David was commanded to play his harp for the king. One day as he played, the tormenting spirit from the Lord once again overcame Saul and he hurled his spear at David. God protected David and the spear stuck into the wall as David fled into the night.

When David arrived home and told his wife, Michal, what had happened, she insisted that he escape that very night. She carried out a daring plan. First, Michal helped him escape through a window while Saul's troops guarded the front entrance waiting for David to emerge through the door. Next, she put an idol in David's bed, covered the head with goat's hair, and the body with blankets. Finally, she lied to the troops, telling them that David was too sick to get out of bed. The plan was successful and God protected David.

Day 1

Reference I Samuel 21-25

Saul relentlessly pursued David and tried to kill him 16 times. List the examples that you found.

Write a brief recap of a time the Lord protected you or someone you know.

My husband was a traveling salesman for many years and often left home on Monday after lunch, drove late into the evening, and was on the job Tuesday morning. One night I was suddenly awakened with an overwhelming sense that I needed to pray for my husband's safety. Looking at the clock, I argued he should be safe in bed. The sense of urgency persisted so I prayed until I felt the Lord's peace and was able to sleep.

He called the next day and I asked him, out of curiosity, when he had arrived at the hotel and explained my late night need to pray for his safety. He said he fell asleep while driving and woke just in time to avoid a semi-truck coming right at him! As we compared times, it was evident that my prayers occurred just as he headed toward the semi! We believe the Lord woke me and insisted I pray for his protection.

Day 2

Read Psalm 59

This Psalm was written after the events in I Samuel 18 and 19.

How does David address God in Psalm 59:1-5?

Who were David's enemies?

What did David ask God to do for him?

In verses 3 and 4 what do we learn about David?

Day 3

Read Psalm 59:6-15

From verses 6 and 7 describe the scene at Michal and David's house.

How did the Lord respond to Saul's plan?

Who is David's God in these verses?

What did David ask God to do to his enemies?

Day 4

Read Psalm 59:14-17

Again, who came to David's house and why?

What is David's song of joy?

Who is David's God in these verses?

Therefore, what did he promise to do?

Day 5

Read Psalms 31

I have never liked the poster with a picture of a terrified kitten clinging to a knotted rope suspended in mid-air and the words "Just tie another knot!" Whenever I see it, I picture myself dangling over the Grand Canyon hanging onto a knotted rope. I know I will quickly lose my grip and fall to my death because I have very little upper body strength. I prefer to picture myself hiding in the shelter of God's presence, not worrying about holding on to a rope or tying another knot to keep above the problems. I see myself just hiding safely in the presence of the Lord!

Psalm 31 is one of the Psalms David wrote when he needed God's protection. David praises God for his answers and gives excellent advice for us.

For what did David specifically pray?

What reasons did David give as to why the Lord should answer him?

Have you ever felt like David? If so how did you respond?

Day 6

Read Psalms 31:9-13

David was in deep trouble. By successfully following orders from his father-in-law, the king, he found himself immensely popular with the people and immensely unpopular with Saul.

Find and record David's vivid description of why he needed God's protection.

I love that David was completely honest with God and told exactly how he felt, no holds barred. Do you think God was surprised about how David felt? Do you think God would be surprised if you told him exactly how you feel?

From the chapter we discover David had confidence to tell God how it was with him. Does this encourage you to tell God exactly how you are feeling and expect him to answer you?

At a time when David wasn't sure he had a future, whom does he trust with it?

What made God's goodness so wonderful for David?

What makes God's goodness real in your life?

For what is David praising the Lord?

Have you ever felt like you and God are cut off from each other?

Explain.

I once heard someone say the silences of the Lord are the hardest test to endure. To me, that means a person is still seeking after God and following his path and it seems as if God has cut him off. I believe this was David's experience expressed in these verses.

Day 7

Reread Psalm 31:21-24

What commands are given?

What areas in your life do you need to be strong and take courage?

What advice do you find in this chapter that you will actively follow?

The Swiss Alps are a beautiful place to live and visit. They are also a very dangerous place when one encounters the frequent storms. At the top of every peak a small chapel is built to shelter the people caught in storms. As soon as a storm hits, the people make their way to the chapel seeking the Lord's protection. As the storm rages, they sense the Lord is with them, sheltering them from the fierce tempest. They experience the presence of the Lord on the top of the mountain and He keeps them safe.

CHAPTER 4

God Directs

I Samuel 22, 23 and Psalm 19, 25

David was on the run from King Saul who heard of supplies the priests gave to David and his men. In a rage, Saul had all of the priests killed. Only Abiathar, a son of Ahimelech, escaped and ran to David who was still trusting God to protect him and help him. David actively asked the Lord to guide him along the best pathway for his life.

While hiding from Saul's threats, David received word that the Philistines were stealing grain from the threshing floor at Keilah, in Judah. He asked the Lord if he should travel there and attack the thieving Philistines.

The Lord's replied, "Yes."

David told his men the plan but they protested. They were afraid to be in Judah much less travel through the land to fight the entire Philistine army.

David went to the Lord and asked him if they should go and fight. The Lord repeated that they should go and he would help them defeat the army.

This encouraged David and his men. They obeyed and had a great victory at Keilah where they slaughtered the Philistines, took their livestock and rescued the Keilahian people. Abiathar accompanied the troops taking the ephod along so he could receive answers from the Lord. Saul heard David was in the walled city of Keilah. He was very excited and told his men that God had handed his enemy over to him and that his nemesis would soon be eliminated. Saul readied all his troops and marched to end his vendetta.

David learned of Saul's plan and told Abiathar to bring the ephod and ask the Lord what he should do. David told the Lord what was going on in his life. He asked if the people he just saved would betray him to Saul.

The Lord said, "Yes."

Not wanting to believe the answer, David asked the Lord again, "Will they hand me over to Saul?"

The Lord's answer remained the same.

Being very wise, David and his six hundred men left Keilah and began to wander through the harsh wilderness. Saul continued hunting David relentlessly.

Day 1

From I Samuel 22, 23

What did David ask of the Lord?

How did David seek God's answers?

What is an ephod?

How does God show us his pathways today?

Share a time God has shown you the path for your life.

Day 2

Read Psalm 25

List qualities David ascribes to God.

List God's promises

To whom are these promises given?

What steps are you willing to take so you qualify?

Day 3

Psalm 25 was one of David's prayers written about the time he lived out the events in 1 Samuel 23.

What were his requests?

What were his praises?

What were the promises he claimed?

What does David's example teach about praying for God's direction for your life?

Submit the direction of your life to the Lord by writing your own Psalm of submission.

Day 4

Read Psalm 19

How did David seek God's direction according to this Psalm?

According to this chapter, how does God speak?

Was this song written for a select group of people?

Compare this Old Testament message to Romans 1:18-20.

God desires to direct men and women around the world along the best pathway for their lives. The best pathway begins with a personal relationship with him through his son, Jesus. When the world was created, the heavens began declaring the glories of the Lord. They speak without words, shouting his existence. The sun is like a radiant bridegroom after his wedding. It rejoices like a great athlete eager to do his job. The main 'job' for the sun and the rest of the heavens is to point men and women around the world to the powerful and magnificent God, The Great I Am, who wants to be their Redeemer and Guide.

Day 5

Read Psalm 19

List different words David used to reference God's Word.

According to a dictionary, what do each of them mean?

In what ways are they the same and what ways are they different?

Day 6

Read Psalm 19:12-14,

How does David address God in this Psalm?

What does David ask God to do for him?

Think about what you know those names to mean. This week, depending on what you are requesting, address God in your prayers by his different names.

Meditate on verse 14. How would your life, and the lives of your family, be enriched if you prayed this?

Day 7

According to Psalm 19 what does God use to direct you and me?

According to this Psalm what ways does God speak to mankind?

What does an individual need to do to capitalize or take advantage of God's desire to be active in their lives?

I often travel in unfamiliar territory for business and frequently find myself going in the wrong direction. On one such occasion, while working in a government installation, I mistakenly took a wrong road and wound up in a top-secret area with a loaded gun pointed at me. The weapon pointed at me made it abundantly clear that I had definitely taken a wrong turn. It was also very clear I had two choices: I could disregard the guard's warnings and charge ahead or I could go back, turn around, and head in the right direction.

Sometimes God's word is like armed guards warning us we are going in the wrong direction. We can heed the warnings, turn our life around and be safe, or we can ignore the warnings and suffer the consequences.

If I had refused the warning of the guards, the consequences would have meant at the least being arrested, and at the worst being killed. Failing to heed the warnings given by God's Word can lead to equally devastating consequences. Let you and me be smart and seek the path God wants us to walk, asking him, through prayer and his word, to point out the right road to follow. Let's put our hope in him and his directions.

CHAPTER 5

God Avenges

I Samuel 24, 26 and Psalm 94

Twice David had opportunity, motive, and peer pressure to eliminate the man who relentlessly pursued him and chose not to do so. Why? He knew God had chosen Saul and it was not his prerogative to do so.

Saul and three thousand of his special troops pursued David into the wilderness of En-Gedi. Saul "happened" to choose the very cave David and his men were hiding to relieve himself.

David's men were very excited and encouraged David to act, and kill Saul. David crept silently to where Saul's robe was and cut off some of the hem. His conscience bothered him and he told his men, "It is a very serious thing to attack the Lord's anointed one, for the Lord himself has chosen him." He refused to allow anyone to harm Saul in any way.

Some time after this, Saul found out through Ziphian messengers that David was hiding on Hakilah Hill. Saul and his troops took off to hunt down this dangerous threat to the king. David heard of his coming so he sent spies to keep apprised of their movements.

One night David personally went to check Saul's encampment. He found Saul and his general, Abner, surrounded by warriors all sound asleep. David determined to get a closer look and asked for volunteers to go into the camp. Abishai decided it was an offer he couldn't refuse, so he stepped to the front of the line. Together he and David snuck into Saul's camp. When they saw Saul and his mighty warriors in slumber with Saul's own spear stuck in the ground near his head, a perfect plan unfolded for Abishai. He told David, "Look at this! We can kill Saul with his own spear!" He further encouraged David by telling him that God had certainly delivered Saul into their hands. It would be simple!

David's answer was an emphatic "No!" Again David knew that God would take care of Saul in his own time and in his own way. It was not his responsibility or right to take his revenge on Saul. So he and Abishai took Saul's spear and water jug and crept out of the camp. No one stirred. When they were safely out of the camp, David shouted for the men to wake up.

David called to Abner, Saul's commander of the troops and asked him why he wasn't taking better care of his King. Then he showed him the King's water jug and spear.

Saul woke up and wanted to know if it was indeed David talking.

David shouted, "Yes!" Then he asked Saul why he was hunting him. David said he could understand if Saul had been directed by God to kill him; but if it was his idea well…stop hunting him.

Saul confessed his sin against David promising to no longer hunt him down.

David showed Saul his water jug and spear and told him to have someone come and get them. He told Saul it was God's responsibility to decide what to do with each of them in regard to who was loyal and right. He reminded Saul he could have killed him twice but was unwilling to lift a finger against God's anointed one.

Saul then blessed David and wished him success.

Day 1

Referencing the story of Saul and David's conflict throughout I Samuel. What in their history gave Saul reason to relentlessly hunt David with every intention of killing him?

Why didn't David kill Saul when twice God delivered him into his hands?

In a practical sense, was David wise or not?

Why do you feel this way?

Day 2

Read Psalm 94

List any names for God that you find.

Who is David's God in this chapter?

Have you ever watched little children playing together? Have you ever watched them when something goes awry and one of them gets angry and starts hitting, biting, or shouting at the other? The responses of the children involved depend on a variety of factors and they respond in a variety of ways. Some get instant satisfaction by retaliating. Others patiently wait until a more convenient time when it is "safer" for them to avenge the wrong done to them. Some of them will retreat into themselves and do nothing but silently or openly cry. Still others will run to their parents as their safe harbor and avenger. As adults, we are not immune to people attacking us for no reason. Like David and the children, we choose how we will respond.

Think about your life and how you have responded in the past to people who have hurt you emotionally and/or physically. Ask God to be your avenger in these circumstances.

Day 3

Read Psalm 94:1-7,

How does David address God?

What does he ask of God?

How does David's prayer help you as you address God?

In what way does his prayer change the way you pray?

Day 4

Read Psalm 94:7-11

What were people saying about God?

How did David respond to these allegations?

Do some today think God is dead or doesn't care?

How do David's words refute those thoughts?

Day 5

Read Psalms 94:12-18

Do you want to be a happy person?

According to these verses what steps does one need to take to be happy?

What is God's part in making you happy?

Who will have a reward?

Day 6

Read Psalms 94:16-19

Who is David's God in these verses?

What questions does David ask in these verses?

How does he answer those questions?

Express a time you had similar questions.

Day 7

Read Psalm 94:20-23

What question does David ask?

Who is David's God?

What are the consequences of being a sinful and evil person?

David knew God would act as his avenger. He knew he should not take revenge on God's anointed man, King Saul. However, he was still in danger due to the king's actions, still being emotionally hurt, and still suffering mentally from the continual pursuit of Saul's army.

It is significant that at the end of his conversation with God, recorded in chapter 94 of Psalms, David remembers God is his rock and his fortress.

Like David, "God's Anointed," or other Christians often hurt us. We are told revenge is God's job, not ours. We can learn from David's example and trust God to be our avenger while we wait and trust God to be our fortress.

CHAPTER 6

God Knows

I Samuel 25 Psalm 37

God has many qualities. Some of them we all recognize and speak of, such as love. One of the more difficult ones for many to deal with is the reality that God is just and judges men and women according to his standard, not ours. The story of Nabal, a mean and dishonest man, and his wife Abigail, a sensible beautiful woman, shows us this side of God.

Nabal and Abigail's story became part of David's story near Carmel, Maon. David sent 10 young men to Nabal asking him for any provisions that he could spare. His reasoning was that his men had not bothered any of Nabal's 3000 sheep or any of his 1000 goats. David assumed because it was sheep shearing time and a time of celebration, he would certainly not refuse his request.

Nabal had a different reaction. He emphatically refused on no uncertain terms and questioned who David thought he was.

When David's messengers told him that Nabal refused, he armed 400 of his men, left 200 to guard the camp, and set off to kill Nabal.

One of Nabal's servants hurried to Abigail and informed her what her husband had done. He filled her in on the details of how David and his men had never harmed them. While they shared the wilderness with them, they acted as a wall of protection around the camp. He warned her that her husband's reaction would lead to trouble if she did not think of something fast.

She quickly gathered 200 loaves of bread, 2 skins of wine, 5 dressed sheep, almost a bushel of grain and 200 fig cakes, and loaded it all onto a donkey. She told the servant to take them to David's camp. She didn't tell Nabal anything of her plan. Then she mounted her donkey and rode off to find David.

When she saw David approaching she dismounted and bowed low at his feet. She accepted all blame and told him her husband lived up to the meaning of his name, "Fool." She asked him to forgive her and gave him the gifts she brought. She pleaded her case very well.

When she finished, David praised the Lord for sending her to him. Without her intervention, David would have killed Nabal's entire household. He told her to go in peace and accepted the gifts.

Abigail returned home to find that Nabal had thrown a big party and was very drunk. She wisely decided to wait until the next morning to tell him of her deed. When he was sober and heard the news, he grew so angry he had a stroke. Ten days later the Lord struck him and he died.

Upon hearing of Nabal's death David asked Abigail to be his wife and she accepted.

Day 1

According to I Samuel 25, what was the result of God's judgment of Nabal?

If you have time, read the entire case Abigail makes to David in verses 26-31. How did David respond?

How do you think God judged Abigail?

What of Abigail's characteristics could we emulate?

Day 2

Read Psalm 37 and fill in the chart.

Consequences of Wickedness	Words to Describe Godly people	Benefits of being a Godly Person
Ps 37:1-8		
Ps 37:9-16		
Ps 37:17-24		
Ps 37:25-32		
Ps 37:33-40		

Day 3

Read Psalms 37:1-8

I love Psalm 37 because it contains many promises and some have been a part of my history with the Lord for years. One of those promises is found in verse four. "Take delight in the Lord, and he will give you your heart's desire." (NLT)

We were looking for a house to buy in Arizona and I couldn't find anything comparable to the home I was leaving. We finally settled on one that met all of our requirements concerning bedrooms, pool, horse privileges and a beautiful yard. However, it lacked the necessary ingredient to make me love it. My husband told me we could sell it anytime and move to something I "loved."

Ten years later I found my dream house! I was determined to buy it. My prayer the night I found "The House" went something like this: "Dear Lord, I do delight in you, you have promised to give me the desires of my heart. My heart's desire is to have this house. Now please work out the details to make it happen. Amen." I went to bed full of excitement wondering how the Lord was going to answer my prayer.

I woke up in the morning and could not believe the miracle that occurred! God changed the desire of my heart! I walked around a house I never loved, now full of love! I saw different aspects I never appreciated before. For example, my family room was very long and narrow and I never totally liked it. That day, I saw it a totally different way. The beautiful fireplace drew me to look beyond the shape and it suddenly became a room I loved!

I continually marvel that the God who created the universe cares enough about a housewife and mother's heart to change her desire and conform it to his will for her family.

List the promises you found.

What advice does David give to his readers?

Day 4

Read Psalms 37:9-16

List the promises of God you found.

What characteristics of God did you find?

Walking is one of the first accomplishments my children and grand-children have achieved. My daughter Kathi and I eagerly waited for the day her son Zak would just do it! One night, when he had decided the time was right, he set off walking between us. We joyfully cheered his every step. When he stumbled, we were ready to catch him. We were all very excited and none more than Zak himself. At one point in his early walking journey, he stopped in the middle of the room, put his hand over his mouth, lit up the room with his grin and filled it with his giggles.

God delights in directing our steps just as we delighted in directing Zak's.

I challenge you right now to follow Zak's example. Stop in the middle of your walk with the Lord, put your hand over your mouth, giggle out loud and recognize the joy walking with the Lord brings you.

Day 5

Read Psalms 37:17-24

What characteristics of God did you find in these verses?

What are God's promises?

How can you apply these promises to your life today?

Day 6

Read Psalm 37:25-32

In what ways do these verses remind you of the story of Nabal and Abigail?

What advice is given in these verses?

List the promises you found.

Write about a time you realized these promises were true in your walk with the Lord.

Day 7

Read Psalms 37:33-40

Who is David's God in these verses?

What promises are given and to whom are they given?

Don't you love this chapter? I do!! Tell God why.

CHAPTER 7

God Listens

I Samuel 21, 27 and Psalm 34, 57

Jonathon, King Saul's son was David's best friend, and confirmed his father wanted to kill David. They knew David needed to leave the city for his protection, so off to Nod to the priest Ahimelech, David went. Ahimelech was not thrilled to see him. In fact he was very fearful and wanted to know why David was alone. David told him he was on a private matter for the king and wanted to know if he had any food. After ascertaining David was ceremonially clean, the priest gave him holy bread: the Bread of the Presence.

David left the palace in such a hurry, but he also needed a weapon. When he found the only available weapon was Goliath's sword, he gladly took it. He then left for Gath and King Achish.

The officers of King Achish were not happy to see him. They asked, "Isn't this David, the king of the land? Isn't he the one the people honor with dancing and singing saying Saul has killed his thousands and David his tens of thousands?"

Fear seized David not knowing what King Achish would do. His solution was to pretend insanity by scratching on doors and letting his spittle run down his beard. King Achish's had his men ask David to leave the country. He felt he had enough crazy people around and didn't need more.

David left Gath and went to a cave in Adullam. Soon a band of men who were also in trouble joined him. It didn't take long for his troops to number about four hundred. Later his father and mother also joined him.

After David spared Saul's life the second time, he began thinking of his personal safety. He decided the best option was to escape the region and seek refuge among the Philistines. He took six hundred men, went again to Gath, and gained the protection of King Achish. When Saul found out where David was he stopped hunting him. In all, Saul tried to kill David sixteen times.

Day 1

Read Psalm 34

Look up the meaning of pretend. Describe the difference between pretending and lying?

What made David fearful?

What was David's formula for living without fear?

What fears do you have that you would like God to take away?

What do think would happen if you asked God to take away your fears?

Day 2

Read Psalm 34:1-10

What advice does David give to those who are discouraged?

What promises are given in these verses?

According to David, what evidence do we have that God listens to our cries for help?

Discouragement comes to each of us with different faces. For David, Saul was the face of discouragement. Even though David was obedient to God and the king, Saul was continuously out to kill him. Whatever our face of discouragement, we can be helped when we follow the advice David gave in these verses.

Day 3

Read Psalm 34:11-14

These verses are packed with excellent advice as we live life in the fast lane. List the advice David gives.

How does this advice fit in your life?

What advice will you emulate?

Day 4

Read Psalm 34:15-22

What does God promise to the righteous: those who do right?

What is God's reaction to those who do evil?

How does God respond to those who are broken hearted?

Day 5

Read Psalm 57

This Psalm was written as David was hiding from Saul in a cave. Have you ever felt like David did in this chapter? For no justifiable reason, Saul relentlessly pursued David with the sole purpose of killing him. Sometimes we want to go into hiding to protect ourselves.

What can we learn from David's example?

What did David ask God to do for him?

What did God do?

Day 6

Read Psalm 57:4-8

How does David describe his situation?

How did David handle it?

What was the condition of David's heart?

Day 7

Read Psalm 57:8-11

Why do you think that he told his soul to awake in verse 8?

Therefore, David began to praise the Lord. Who did he want to be his audience?

What words did he use?

Who is David's God in this chapter?

Throughout Psalms, The Passion Translation uses the phrase "Pause in his Presence" instead of "Selah." Many times as I write this study, I pause in his presence and listen for his voice. I think David during his hiding time, was "Pausing in God's Presence," listening, praising and seeking his ways. I highly recommend doing the same when you need to escape difficult times

CHAPTER 8

God Keeps Promises

I Samuel 31-II Samuel 5, and Psalms 13, 27 and 97

David is finally free from his enemy, Saul. First, crack Philistine archers killed three of Saul's sons including Jonathan, David's best friend. Then one got close enough to King Saul to shoot and gravely wound him. When Saul realized how badly he was injured, he begged his armor bearer to kill him. He refused, so Saul fell on his own sword, killing himself.

David received word of Saul's death and the death of his sons from an Amalekite. He told David he came upon the gravely wounded Saul who begged him to be put out of his misery. He claimed to fulfill the desire of King Saul by killing the Lord's anointed. David was livid that someone dared kill the King. He immediately had one of his men kill the Amalekite. He and his men mourned the loss of Saul and his sons. You can read the beautiful funeral song David composed for them in II Samuel 1:17-27

David once again asked the Lord what he should do. The Lord instructed him to go to Hebron in Judah. The leaders of Judah came to him and anointed him King of Judah. Meanwhile in Israel, Abner, the commander and chief of Saul's army, appointed Saul's son Ishbosheth, as King of Israel. As you might imagine the two Kings did not become instant friends. In reality, the war between the house of David and the house of Saul just took on a new look, and became the war between Judah and Israel. Joab led Judah's troops and Abner led Israelite troops.

When Ishbosheth accused Abner of infidelity, he became enraged and threatened to help David become king over Israel too. Upon hearing of Abner's possible defection, David sent word that he wanted his wife, Michal back (she had been given to another man after David fled Saul's household). Ishbosheth agreed that the dowry of two hundred Philistines merited her return so she was taken from her husband, Palti, and given back to David.

Abner traveled to Hebron and pledged his support of David. He entertained Abner and twenty of his men. They asked David to let them go back to Israel where they would rally the people to crown David as king over all Israel.

When Joab returned from the raid and found out Abner had come and gone in safety, he became very angry. He sent messengers to bring Abner back to Hebron so he could talk to him privately. Instead of talking to him, Joab took him aside and murdered him. David was very upset and mourned the death of Abner. He told the people that even though he was king he could not control Joab and his brother Abishai, they were too strong. Therefore, he wanted the Lord to repay them for their evil.

Ishbosheth lost all courage when he heard Abner had been murdered. His followers became paralyzed with fear. Maybe it was at this time that two brothers, Baanah and Rechab, captains of the king's raiding parties, began to plot the death of Ishbosheth. One day about noon, the king and his doorkeeper were taking a little nap. The brothers snuck into the bedroom and stabbed Ishbosheth in the stomach. After they cut off his head, they took it to David. They were expecting him to be pleased and give them a reward. Instead, David was not happy and had them killed.

All the tribes of Israel went to Hebron to meet with David. They acknowledged that David had been the true leader of Israel even while Saul was alive. They proclaimed the Lord had anointed him shepherd of the people of Israel. Together they made a covenant before the Lord and the leaders anointed him king over all Israel.

Day 1

Read I Chronicles 10:13-14

Why did Saul die?

What was David's reaction to the death of Saul?

What does David's reaction to the death of all his enemies tell you about his character?

Day 2

Read Psalm 78:70-72

Who turned Saul's kingdom over to David?

Who came to Hebron?

What did they say about David?

In II Samuel 5:6-10 who marched to Jerusalem what happened?

Day 3

Read Psalm 13

Why do you think David was hurting?

What questions does David ask?

What does David demand of God?

What does David want his God to do?

What did David celebrate and how did he celebrate?

Day 4

Read Psalm 27

Describe David's emotional state in verses Psalm 27:1-4.

What did David want more than anything?

How close did David say he wanted to be to God?

Where does God hide David?

Where would one find David when trouble came?

Day 5

Read Psalm 27

According to Psalm 27: 5-6 what did God do for David? How does David respond?

What did David ask God to do for him?

What were the requirements for God to answer?

Think about this Psalm in relationship to your life. What will or should you do to emulate David?

Day 6

Read Psalm 97

Who is David's God in this chapter?

Describe God's throne.

What part do the heavens play in God's story?

What are God's people to hate and why?

What instructions are given to those who love God?

Day 7

Read Psalm 97

According to Psalm 97:11, what seeds are planted in those who love God?

Why should those who love God be glad and give thanks?

What promises does God give to those who love him?

What promises do you find in Psalms 13, 27 and 97 that you need fulfilled in your life today

God is Celebrated

II Samuel 6, I Chronicles 13-16 and Psalm 105:1-15

David was finally king of Judah and Israel and made Jerusalem his capital. When David decided to bring the Ark to the City of David he had a special tent made for it. The Ark was made per God's instructions including what was to be put inside and how it was to be moved. The Ark of the Covenant was a symbol of God's Presence when Moses was leading the people to the Promised Land.

David commissioned thirty thousand troops to bring the Ark to Jerusalem. He instructed two brothers Uzzah and Ahio to guide the Ark that rested on top of a cart made for the transport. As David and a large crowd followed, they celebrated to the Lord with musical instruments, singing and dancing.

When they got to the threshing floor belonging to Nacon, the oxen stumbled and Uzzah reached out to steady the Ark. God struck Uzzah dead. David at first became angry with the Lord and them became afraid and wondered how he would get the Ark to Jerusalem. He decided to leave it with Obed-Edom's family.

After three months David decided to try and move it one more time. This time he talked with God and asked his opinion on how to move it. God told him that only the Levites should be involved in its movement. David summoned the elite priests and told them to purify themselves in preparation for the adventure of a lifetime. A few good men were selected for the honor of carrying the Ark on their shoulders using the poles that were threaded through the rings on the side of the Ark. Finally, David instructed Levites to hand pick musicians and singers to accompany the Ark.

Once again the Ark of God was on its way to a new home. The journey began with lots of celebrating and singing and dancing and shouting and trumpet blowing. This time before they had gotten very far, they stopped and David sacrificed a fatted calf and an ox. David led the way into his capital. He was extremely happy and acted like a fanatic for the Lord with much singing and dancing.

Michal, David's wife, watched and was not happy with his display of extreme exuberance. She was disgusted and told him he acted in a manner unbecoming to the King.

David replied to her complaints with words like these, "I am dancing before the Lord, who chose me above your father and your family. He appointed me as leader of Israel, God's chosen people. So I am willing to act like a fool in order to show my joy in the Lord. Yes and I am even willing to look more foolish than this." (NLT)

Day 1

Read I Chronicles 15:25-16:7

Describe the events that happened in I Chronicles 15:25-29

What do you think of Michal's response?

Describe the events that happened in verses I Chronicles 16:1-7.

Who is David's God in these verses?

Day 2

Read I Chronicles 16.

I Chronicles 16:8-36 is a song David composed especially for the occasion of the moving to the Ark. List ways David proclaims those who love God should respond in celebration of God.

There are many sporting events where sports fanatics express enthusiasm for their team. How do those who are fans for the Lord behave?

Michal thought David was a fanatic for the Lord. What do you think it means to be a fanatic for the Lord today?

Day 3

Read and compare the following passages:

	I Chronicles 16:8-22	Psalms 105:1-15
What instructions are given?		
Who is the Lord?		

Day 4

Read and compare the following passages:

	I Chronicles 16:23-33	Psalms 96
How are the people to praise the Lord and why?		
What else is to praise the Lord?		

Day 5

Read and compare the following passages:

	I Chronicles 16:34-35	Psalms 106: 1, 47-48
What requests are made?		
Why should we give thanks to God?		
What is the conclusion of each of these verses?		

Day 6

Read Psalm 100

(I enjoy reading this passage from The Message, which is available online.)

People in America celebrate many things: weddings, graduations, births and winning. Every celebration includes happy joyous people. I love to celebrate and I especially love to celebrate God. I love to experience a joyous celebration with my Bible study gals. After I discovered these wonderful words in the Message, I began practicing doing what we are told to do. "On your feet now-applaud God! Bring a gift of laughter, and sing your selves into his presence." We stand and clap for God and yell yea God! We cannot keep from smiling and laughing as we celebrate God.

How does this chapter tell us to celebrate God?

List things in your life you want to shout praises of celebration for God.

What promises did God give his people in verse 5?

Day 7

Read Psalm 66

Psalm 66 is another chapter that tells us to applaud God. Have you ever thought about applauding God? Thoughtfully reflect on how you can obey the advice in this chapter.

First identify advice given in this chapter.

What happens to our enemies when we follow these directives?

How does the earth respond?

How do you respond to God's wonders?

What should cause us to sing?

From verses 8-12 list the reasons we should give him a thunderous welcome.

I have experienced, like David, the reality of verses 16-20 in my life. Like David I believed God listened to my call because I wasn't cozy with evil. Instead, he listened and came on the double when he heard my prayer. Reread this amazing chapter and list the reasons you found to celebrate and give God your applause.

CHAPTER 10

God Forgives

II Samuel 11-12 and Psalm 32, 51

David's whole life reads like a Hollywood movie and his encounter with Bathsheba adds the dimension directors are seeking.

Scene 1

It is a lovely spring evening and King David unable to sleep is walking on his roof. His troops are busy fighting the Amorites and really he should have been there too. His eyes see a drop dead beautiful woman taking a bath. He can't stop thinking about her so he makes some inquires and finds out her name is Bathsheba and is married to Uriah, one of his mighty men. He sends for her and

PLAN A: the affair begins.

Scene II

Plan B: It is now a month or so later and David is still at the palace. Bathsheba sends David word that she is going to have his baby. He decides the best course of action is to cover it up.

Scene III

Plan C: David believes since he couldn't resist Bathsheba's beauty, neither will her husband. So he sends for Uriah. He fully expects Uriah to come home and sleep with his wife. However, it isn't in Uriah's character to go to the comfort of his wife while the rest of his troops are still on the battle-field. Instead he sleeps at the palace gates. When David hears that Uriah is still waiting at the gate, he invites him to dinner. David gets Uriah drunk and sends him home to Bathsheba. Once again Uriah refuses to cooperate and spends the night alone.

Scene IV

Plan D: David becomes desperate. He sends Uriah back to the battlefield with a message to Joab the commander in chief of the army. Joab is in-structed to put Uriah the Hittite in the hottest part of the battle and pull back the rest of the troops. The plan works perfectly and Uriah is killed on the front line. After Bathsheba's time of mourning is over she and David were married.

Scene V

Enter Nathan, God's prophet. Nathan tells David a story that goes like this. "A very rich man with lots of money gave a party and wanted to feed his guests. Instead of killing one of his own goats he killed the goat of a man who only had one precious goat that was the family pet." David is livid and declares that the man who did such a terrible thing in his king-dom should be killed. Then Nathan hits David with the truth, he is that man. He continues to tell him that the Lord God is very angry with him and that there will be consequences for his sin. God says "I appointed you king over Israel. I delivered you from Saul and would have given you more. Why did you despise my word by doing evil in my sight? You killed Uriah with a sword and now the sword will constantly be in your household. On top of that, your wives will be raped in broad daylight."

Scene VI

David confesses his sin to Nathan. He is genuinely sorry for sinning against God. God forgives David's sin but doesn't remove the conse-quences. All the things Nathan tells David will happen do happen, and in addition the baby Bathsheba is pregnant with dies.

Day 1

Read Psalm 51

Psalm 51 was written after Nathan confronted David's adultery with Bathsheba and murder of Uriah. David knew God's view of his actions and that God's judgments were right and fair. I often thought the baby's death was very harsh punishment until I was comforted by David's response in this Psalm.

As you read through this amazing chapter of God's redeeming love for David, look for a verse or several verses that express your life's experience when you received God's forgiveness.

List the names for God you found.

What characteristic did you find?

Day 2

Read Psalm 51:1-6

How long had David been a sinner?

Who did David claim he had sinned against?

What was his prayer?

Day 3

Read Psalm 51:7-15

Find and record at least 15 for which David prays.

What did the King promise he would do after God answered his prayer?

What do these verses challenge you to do?

Day 4

Read Psalm 51:16-19

What does God want from his people?

Define a broken spirit.

When will God rejoice?

Day 5

Read Psalm 32

Psalm 32 is a wonderful Psalm. David wrote this one to commemorate his forgiveness. It gives clear and powerful instructions as a template to use to receive God's forgiveness.

According to David, what are the instructions to receive God's forgiveness?

Compare verses 1 and 2 with Romans 4:5-8

A few years ago I was in a Bible study and one of the members declared that repentance was just an Old Testament doctrine. How do the above passages refute that wrong theology?

Day 6

Read Psalm 32

Who are happy and fulfilled people?

How does anyone get blessed and relief?

Describe David's life before he confessed his sin.

According to verse 5 what is required in order for David to receive God's forgiveness?

What did David learn through this experience?

What promises are given to believers who confess their sins when God exposes them?

Sometimes, like in David's case, he uses people. Pause in his presence and let God expose any hidden sin in your life. Confess it and receive the gift of forgiveness.

Day 7

Read Psalm 32

Who is David's God?

What did David hear God say to him?

What did David conclude?

Contrast one who resists God with one who trusts in the Lord.

How are the forgiven to react to God's goodness?

Many years ago my father and I had a conversation about my hero David. He was unimpressed as David was an imperfect sinner not worthy of my admiration. I did not know how to respond. I said nothing. I prayed for God to give me another chance to talk with my dad about this issue.

It took a few years before my dad brought up the subject that all those heroes were sinners. This time God answered my prayer and gave me this reply: Yes David sinned but he repented. My dad quietly reflected on what was said. It took a few more years before Dad, like David, repented. He asked Jesus to be his Savior.

I pray that each of you will think about this wonderful picture of God's salvation plan and follow David and my dad's example to repent and ask God to forgive you. Then praise him for forgiving you and when the door is open share what he has done for you.

Which of these action steps do you need to leap into doing?

-Repenting

-Accepting Jesus offered forgiveness

-Praising God

-Tell others about God's Good News

CHAPTER 11

God Says No

I Chronicles 17-22 and Psalm 72, 89

David talked to God's Prophet, Nathan and expressed his desire to build a house for God. He thought it would be appropriate as he was living in a wonderful palace while God's Ark was in a tent. Nathan told him to go ahead and do it, "for the Lord is with you."

That night the Lord told Nathan, no, David was not the one to build him a house. He was to tell David that he, God, had never lived in a house. Instead he had moved with the children of Israel as they moved. God has never asked for a house. He was to remind David of their history together. He promised that David's name would be famous and that he, God, would provide a home for his people. Furthermore, God promised David would have a dynasty that would never end.

David's reaction to God's no; he prayed. He praised God for his promise to make his family a lasting dynasty. He then went and continued to fight many battles. In one of them he and his men captured 1,000 chariots, 7,000 charioteers, 20,000-foot soldiers and crippled most of the horses.

Later he took a census, which displeased God and caused 70,000 people to die with a plague. When David saw the angel of the Lord between heaven and Jerusalem he repented. God told him to build God an altar on this threshing floor and later the Temple would be built here too.

David began to assemble the necessary materials necessary to build a magnificent glorious Temple that would be famous throughout the world. He assembled many and told them that even though he was young and inexperienced, his son Solomon, would be the one to build the Temple.

David summoned Solomon and told him his story. He shared that he had wanted to build a house for God; but God told him NO! He told Solomon that God had told him that because he had killed many men in battle and shed so much blood, he was not the one to build the Temple that honored his name.

God had also told him that his son was a man of peace and Solomon was his name. God promised to grant him peace throughout his lifetime. God also promised to secure the Temple forever.

Day 1

When God told David he was not the one to build him a house what did he do?

What promises did God make to David?

David continued to fight many battles. Besides the battle with yet another giant named Goliath; how else was he successful?

What was the result of the census?

Who was to build the temple?

Why did God tell David he was not the one to build the Temple?

Day 2

Read Psalm 72

Psalm 72 was written by David for Solomon.

What were David's requests for Solomon?

Who will surrender and come to this King?

Who did David declare would serve Solomon?

Verses 18 and 19 to tell us to praise the Lord, what reasons are given?

Day 3

Read Psalm 89

Psalm 89 was written by Ethan, the Ezrahite and is filled with promises from God.

From Psalm 89:1-8, what promise does Ethan make?

Who will be his audience?

What promises does God make to and about David?

What is heaven's inhabitant's reaction to God?

Day 4

Read Psalm 89:9-18.

I love that throughout the Bible there are references to God the Creator. How do these verses highlight the amazing Creator and his creation?

In addition to being the Creator of the universe, what other aspects of God are mentioned?

What are the benefits of worshiping God?

Day 5

Read Psalm 89:19-37

What are the promises that God gave to David and his family?

What warnings are also promised?

How is God addressed in verse 20?

How important to God is it for him to keep his word?

Most, if not all, of the promises God gives in the Bible require us to obey the directions he gives. The Bible is like a recipe book for life with him. When we are using a recipe to make something and we change the amount or exchange one ingredient for another, the outcome is different than the original dish. We very well can wreck the whole thing by not following the directions. Sometimes it only takes substituting a tablespoon of salt for a teaspoon of salt to wreck the entire dish. Sometimes our life with Christ can be like that. It may only take a simple act of disobedience to God's way to forever alter the course of your life and the lives of your family. From David's life we learn the ramifications of his disobedience were long lasting and affected the entire nation, and indeed the world.

Day 6

Read Psalm 89:38-45.

What happened in these verses?

Do you think that these happenings are a result of God's promise being fulfilled?

Why or why not?

Who is David's God in these verses?

Day 7

Read Psalm 89:46-52.

Review the questions Ethan, the author, asks in these verses. Which ones have you asked too?

What did you conclude?

How does this chapter end?

CHAPTER 12

God Sustains

II Samuel 13-21 and Psalm 18

David was a warrior and continued battling almost his entire life. He not only battled the Philistines, but also his son, Absalom

Remember Nathan's promise to David, that because of his sin the sword would be a constant threat in his household.

Absalom was enraged when his half-brother Amnon, raped Absalom's full-sister Tamar. It took two years, but he finally executed his form of justice and had Amnon killed. David was very angry when he heard this news. David went into mourning for his dead son Amnon and Absalom fled to his Grandfather. After a two years David and Absalom were reconciled.

However, Absalom repaid his father's kindness by attempting to steal the hearts of the people from his father. Absalom deceived the King by claiming he needed to go to Hebron and fulfill his vow to the Lord. His real purpose was to stir up a rebellion and depose King David. He was successful. When David heard that the whole country had taken up with Absalom he fled Jerusalem. He took his entire household except ten concubines. Absalom entered the city, took over the palace, set up a tent on the roof and slept with the concubines in full view of everyone.

Absalom asked for advice about pursuing his father. The answer was yes. In the meantime David organized his troops. The troops told him he was much too valuable to go into this battle, so he stood beside the gate and watched as thousands of his men marched by. At the end of the day, twenty thousand of Absalom's troops were killed as well as Absalom. David mourned the death of yet another son.

We will end the story of David's life with yet another battle and another Goliath. It happened this way: War broke out between David's kingdom and the Philistines. When David and his men went out to fight, David became exhausted. David's men told him "No more fighting on the front line for you! Don't snuff out the lamp of Israel."

David's men continued the fight and were able to kill four giants including another Goliath.

Day 1

Read II Samuel 22 and Psalm 18

These chapters contain the same message written after God saved David from all his enemies. As you read and study both chapters, expect to meet a dramatic God who rewards his chosen people.

Use your own words to describe David's life with God.

Who is David's God?

Day 2

Read Psalm 18:6-15.

Verse 6 tells us that David prayed to God, asking for his help. Verses 7-15 tell how God answered that prayer in unbelievable ways.

What was the first thing God did when David prayed?

Which of God's emotions do these verses mention?

As you read these verses what emotions were stirred up in you?

What do they teach you about God?

Reading these verses reminds me of an experience our family had on a trip to the Grand Canyon. A horrendous rainstorm blew in soaking everything in its path, including us. We escaped to the El Tovar Hotel and explored until the rain subsided. When it did, we all went to see the BIG HOLE one more time. We were rewarded with an incredible sight. When we first got to the edge, there were a few clouds within the canyon and very dark rain cloud hanging overhead, but we could still see the bottom. Within a minute the canyon filled with clouds totally obliterating the Grand Canyon. As I snapped away with my camera, I heard others around me talking in hushed tones about the incredible things we had just witnessed.

Day 3

Read Psalm 18:16-24

What did David's enemies do?

What did David's God do for him?

According to these verses David declared himself innocent. Then he went on to tell what he meant by that. What did he say?

What is required for people to enjoy those same benefits?

Day 4

Read Psalms 18:25-36

List the attributes of God.

What did God do for David?

Which of these attributes encouraged you and why?

My wonderful friend, Joyce was diagnosed with terminal cancer. All who knew her were devastated and prayed asking God for a miracle. One day she and I were talking about her illness and I asked what her hardest times were. She told me waking up in the night with the darkness surrounding her was very difficult. I have always loved the Psalms and have read them periodically through my life. Shortly after our conversation, I read chapter 18 and verse 28 encouraged me. I prayed that God would turn Joyce's darkness into light and be her light even the darkness of the night and the darkness of her disease. The next time we talked I asked how her nights were going and she said she was sleeping better and the darkness no longer held the terror it had before. God answered my prayer and made her darkness light.

Day 5

Read Psalm 18:37-50

What did David's God do for him in these verses?

God usually acts through people and he did so in David's life as well. What did he enable David to do?

Who is David's God?

Day 6

Read Psalm 18

How does Psalm 18 enlarge or enhance or enforce your concept of God?

Which of the attributes David praises God for having is the most meaningful to you at this point in your life?

Write a short praise to the Lord thanking him for that characteristic.

A friend asked me why I continue to read and study the Bible. I answered: because it is alive and meets me where I am and supplies what I need to continue to serve him. II Samuel 22 and Psalm 18 are examples of what I mean.

Day 7

Read Psalm 62

I was taking a friend to the airport after he had been visiting my very ill husband. All the way to the airport he verbally beat me up with his advice. I understood that he was looking out for the best interest of his friend, but he told me I was getting old and who was going to take care of my husband if I died, and that I needed to follow his advice. I had talked multiple times with my Advisor, God, and asked him what I should do. God's advice was totally different than our friends.

I came home just emotionally and spiritually spent. I was unwilling to even think. God prompted me to open the Word. I just opened it randomly and it fell open to Psalm 62 in the Message. It is the same message in both Psalm 18 and II Samuel 22. I loved it!!

It contained everything that I needed, even a laugh, "How long will you run with the bullies?" It fed me and encouraged me. It reminded me that God is my one and only; that he is solid rock under my feet; breathing room for my soul; an impregnable castle and I am set for life.

List the ways this passage encourages you today.

In what ways can this Psalm be applied to your life in the coming days?

FINAL NOTE

I hope you have enjoyed this study about David and His God as much as I have enjoyed wrting and teaching it. My desire is that we learn from David's walk with God and follow his example by loving his God more. I also desire that you, like David, would have a personal relationship with his God and have Him be your God too.

David's journey began when God called him from taking care of his father's sheep, to serve as the chosen King of Israel. Like David, God calls us to serve Him. In the book of Revelation 3:20 Jesus says, "Look I stand at the door and knock. If you hear my voice and open the door, I will come in." I would like to ask if you have opened the door of your life so you can serve God through the invitation of Jesus?

David also had to repent of his sins. Psalm 51 is his prayer of repentance. He acknowledged that he sinned against God alone and he had been a sinner since birth and asked God to purify him from his sins so he could be clean. Like David, I invite you to confess to God you are sorry for their sins and ask God to wash you so you can be whiter than snow.

Throughout David's life he wanted to please God and continually sought his advice and then followed it. He praised his God for his continued love and joy as they walked together.

May you, like David, find peace with God as you continually surrender your life in obedience to him.

Glenna Derbyshire

www.ingramcontent.com/pod-product-compliance
Lightning Source LLC
Chambersburg PA
CBHW060238030426
42335CB00014B/1516